Life Cycles on the Farm

FUSION

Life Cycle of a
Sheep

by Noah Leatherland

Bearport Publishing

Minneapolis, Minnesota

Credits

All images are courtesy of Shutterstock.com, unless otherwise specified. With thanks to Getty Images, Thinkstock Photo, and iStockphoto. Cover – tanyaya, YummyBuum, Ekaterina_Mikhaylova, Borodatch, Inna Astakhova. Recurring images – Oleh Svetiukha, uiliaaa, YummyBuum, Terdpong, tanyaya. 2 – Eric Isselee, Heath Johnson, Inna Astakhova. 4 – Dipak Shelare. 4&5 – AJP. 5 – Dernkadel. 6 – photomaster. 7 – Pazargic Liviu. 8 – D. Ribeiro. 9 – Ayesha Wilson. 10 – Pozdeyev Vitaly. 11 – Lina Keil, Melinda Nagy. 12 – Teresa Otto. 13 – Clara Bastian. 14 – Heath Johnson. 15 – Geothea. 16 – Madeleine Cardozo. 17 – Aleksandar Malivuk. 18 – Debbiedao. 19 – Terelyuk. 20 – Denisa V, Borodatch. 21 – Anne Coatesy. 22 – photomaster. 22&23 – Eric Isselee.

Library of Congress Cataloging-in-Publication Data is available at www.loc.gov or upon request from the publisher.

ISBN: 979-8-88916-961-1 (hardcover)
ISBN: 979-8-89232-489-2 (paperback)
ISBN: 979-8-89232-125-9 (ebook)

For more information, write to Bearport Publishing, 5357 Penn Avenue South, Minneapolis, MN 55419.

Contents

WHAT IS A LIFE CYCLE?

All living things go through different stages of life. We come into the world and grow over time. Eventually, we die. This is the life cycle.

As humans, we start life as babies. We grow into toddlers and children. Then, we become teenagers. Finally, we are adults and get even older. We may have babies of our own, and then the cycle begins again.

SHEEP ON THE FARM

Animals on the farm go through life cycles, too. Farm sheep are **domestic** animals. This means they are not wild. People keep them as **livestock**.

There are hundreds of different **breeds** of sheep.

A group of sheep is often called a flock. Some farms have only a few sheep, while others have hundreds or even thousands. Farmers raise these animals for their meat, their milk, and their warm hair called wool.

GETTING READY FOR LAMBS

Female sheep can have babies called lambs. Usually, a **pregnant** sheep has only one baby growing inside her at a time. After about five months, the baby is ready to be born.

A PREGNANT SHEEP
When getting ready to have her baby, the mother sheep may stop eating.

When it is time to give **birth**, the mother sheep finds a spot to be alone. Sometimes, she gives birth by herself. Other times, farmers may need to help get her lamb out.

LITTLE LAMBS

Right after a lamb is born, the mother licks its nose to make sure it can breathe. Then, she licks the rest of the baby clean. A new lamb is able to walk soon after it is born.

A lamb weighs about 12 pounds (5 kg) when it is born.

Lambs have very soft wool that helps them stay warm. But sometimes, their wool isn't enough. Farmers give lambs blankets and small heated boxes to keep them warm.

MOTHER'S MILK

Shortly after being born, a lamb drinks milk from its mother's body. This milk gives the lamb the **nutrients** it needs to have a healthy start to life.

A mother sheep makes different sounds to tell her lamb it's time to drink.

Within a few weeks, the lamb starts nibbling on grass along with drinking milk. After a few months, the lamb switches to eating only solid food, including grasses and grains.

JOINING THE FLOCK

When the little lamb is about four months old, the lamb and its mother joins the rest of the flock. It can take the young sheep a few days to get used to the other sheep on the farm.

Sheep are very social. They have close bonds with others in the flock.

When it is about a year old, the lamb is called a yearling. This is a bit like being a teenager for humans.

RAMS AND EWES

When it is a year and a half old, the sheep is an adult. Adult **male** sheep are called rams. Females are called ewes (YOOZ). Some breeds of sheep grow horns as they get older.

Sheep sometimes use their horns to fight and protect themselves.

Ewes can weigh as much as 400 lb. (180 kg) by the time they are 2 years old. Most ewes have their first lamb at this age.

ALL GROWN UP

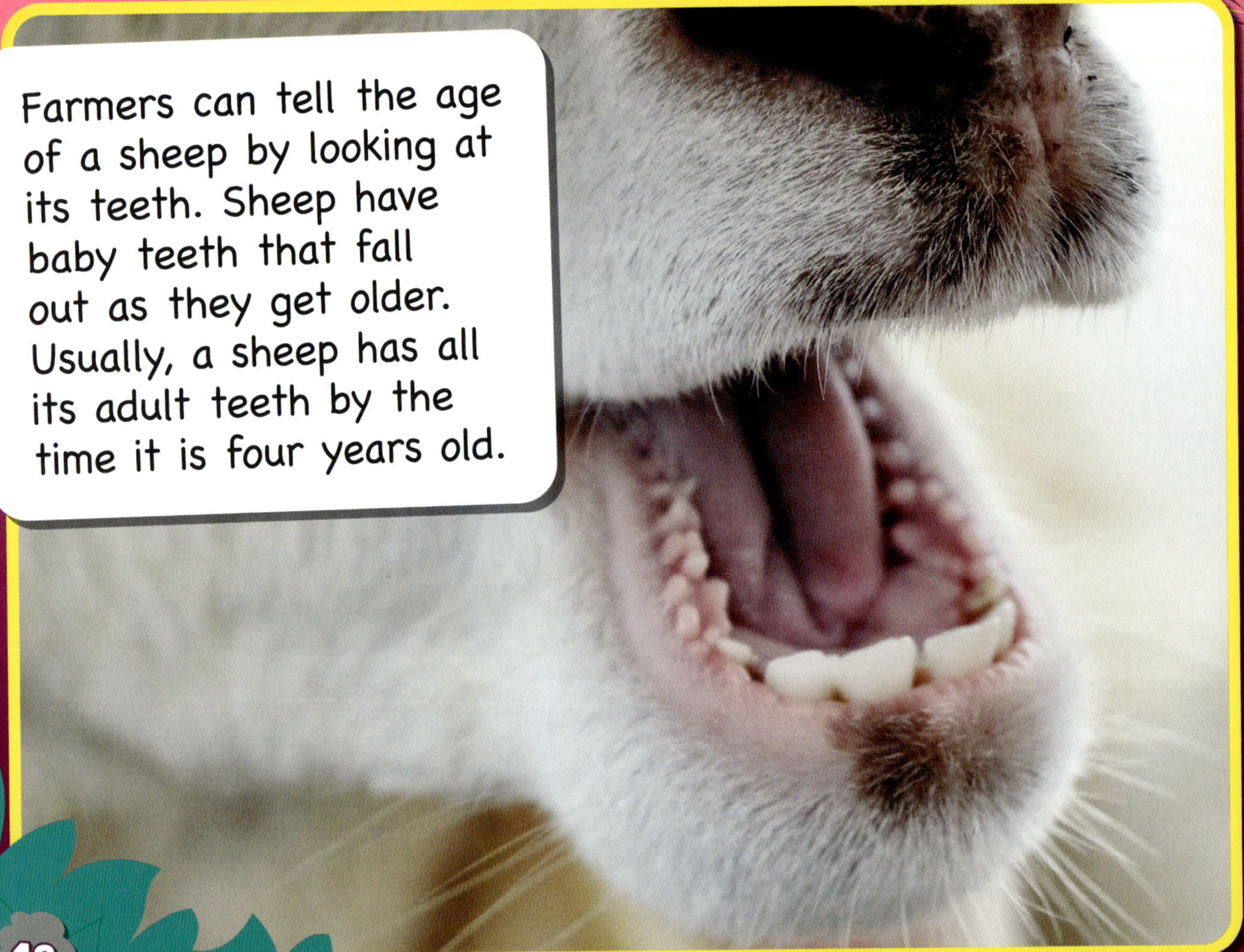

Farmers can tell the age of a sheep by looking at its teeth. Sheep have baby teeth that fall out as they get older. Usually, a sheep has all its adult teeth by the time it is four years old.

Cutting off a sheep's wool keeps the animal from getting too hot.

Cutting off a sheep's wool is called shearing. Lambs have their first shearing when they are one year old. Then, they are usually sheared once a year. This wool can be used to make warm clothes and blankets.

THE END OF LIFE

Sheep have many **predators**, including wolves and coyotes. Farmers build fences and train other animals to **protect** their flocks.

Dogs, donkeys, and llamas are often used to keep the flocks safe.

Sheep can live for about 10 years. However, farm sheep raised for their meat usually don't live this long.

LIFE CYCLE OF A SHEEP

A sheep begins its life as a lamb. The lamb drinks milk from its mother and grows into a yearling. The yearling continues to grow and becomes an adult.

During its life, a sheep may have lambs of its own. Eventually, the sheep will die, but the lambs live on and have even more sheep. This keeps the life cycle going!

Glossary

birth when a female has a baby

breeds different types of an animal

domestic tamed for use by humans

female a sheep that can give birth to young

livestock animals that are raised by people on farms or ranches

male a sheep that cannot give birth to young

nutrients substances needed by plants and animals to grow and stay healthy

predators animals that hunt and eat other animals

pregnant when a female animal has babies growing inside her

protect to keep safe from harm

Index